the art of G.R. SANTOSH

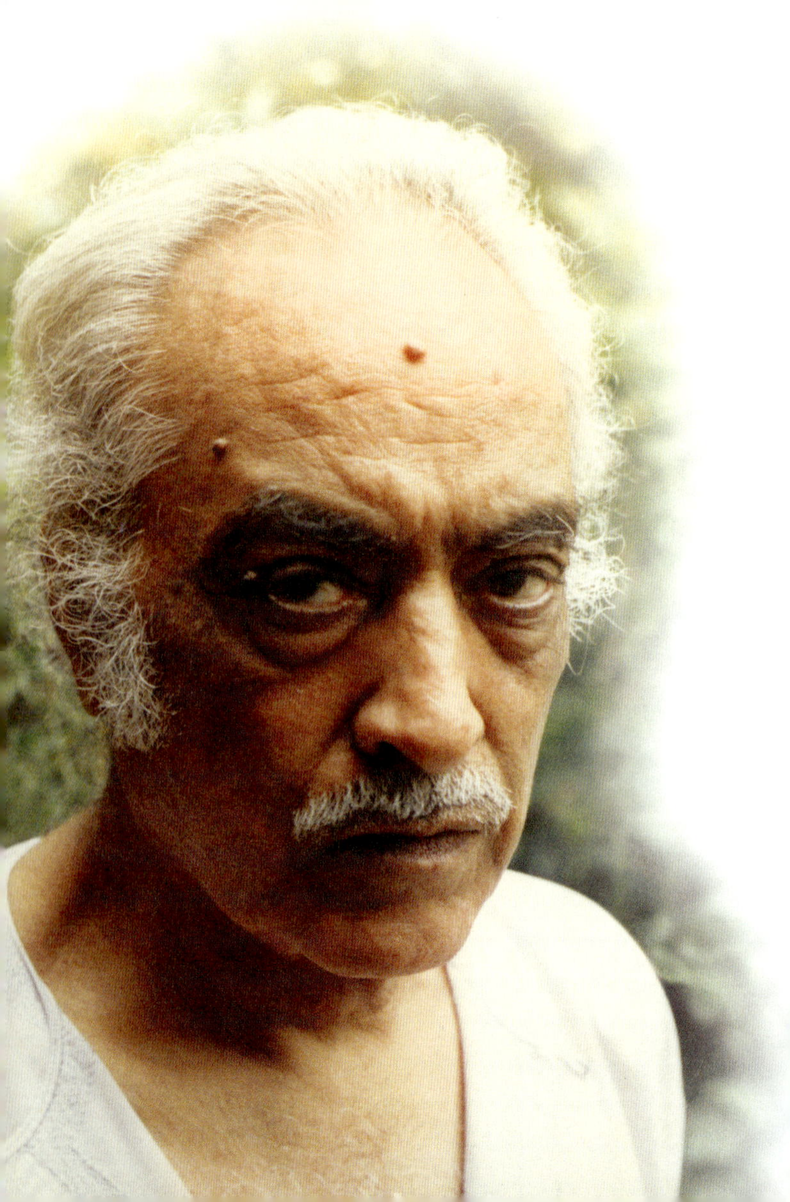

the art of G.R. SANTOSH

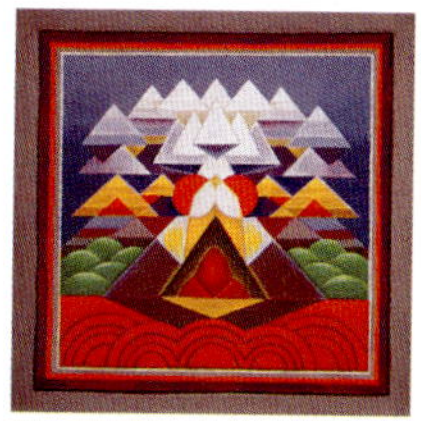

Shantiveer Kaul

Lustre Press
Roli Books

Born Ghulam Rasool Dar in 1929 at Chinkral Mohalla, Habbakadal, in the heart of Srinagar city of Kashmir in a lower middle class Shia Muslim family, Santosh had to give up his education while he was still a boy owing to the death of his father – a policeman. His early years were full of struggle. Being the eldest son, he had to work variously as a sign-board painter, a *papier-mache* worker and a weaver to make a living and support his family. But even at that time he knew and understood his destiny. With whatever little money he could save he bought colour for painting, his love and passion right from childhood. His environment was steeped in a refined understanding of the arts and marked by a non-orthodox, yet deeply pious outlook. This, in fact, is the quintessence of traditional Kashmiri ethos. All his life Santosh remained a traditional Kashmiri at heart with a modern, liberal mind. His modern and liberal

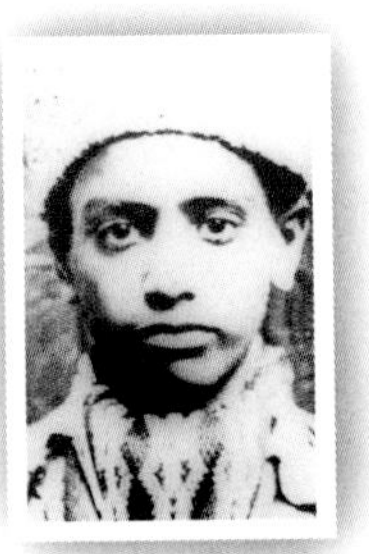

The young Santosh.

outlook is evidenced by the fact that right at the beginning of his marriage he took on the name of his wife – Santosh – as his *nom de plume* and made it his very own. She, in turn, came to be known as Toshi.

Early on, he learnt to paint landscape in watercolour from Dina Nath Raina. In 1952, he became a member of the Progressive Artists' Association, a group of young artists who were influenced by progressive thought and yet wanted to be Modernists. They were much impressed by the works of Cezanne and the Cubists. In the early landscapes of Santosh there are unmistakable echoes of the Cubists, especially Picasso. In 1954, Santosh went to Maharaja Sayajirao University, Baroda, on a scholarship and studied for two years as a non-collegiate student under Prof N.S. Bendre, the renowned artist from Bombay, who was then the Head of the Art

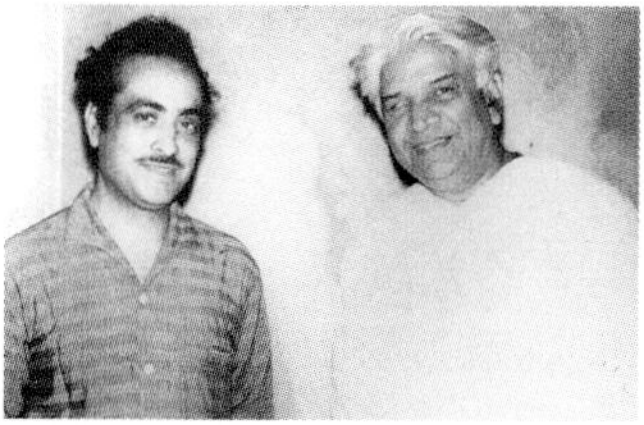

With Prof N.S. Bendre (right).

Department at the University. Here he perfected the art of figure drawing and portraiture in which he was to later excel. During his sojourn at Baroda he produced a host of work, both figurative as well as landscape, mainly in the Cubist style. The subject of his landscapes was almost always Kashmir. He returned to Kashmir in 1956 and continued to paint in the Cubist vein till 1959.

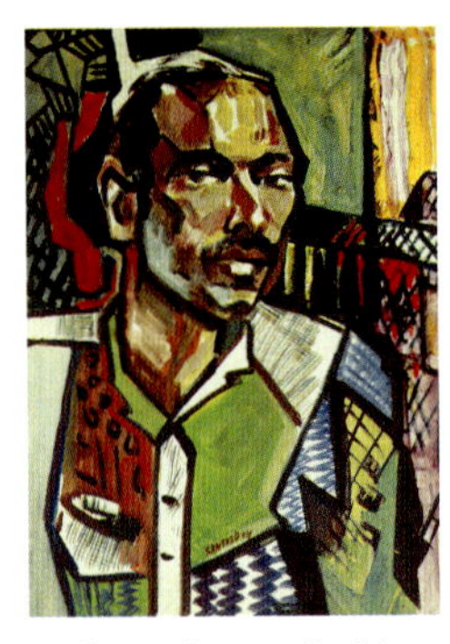

Santosh excelled in figure drawing.

Between 1959 and 1964 Santosh's art began to evolve into a more individual idiom. He experimented successfully, with the impasto (the process of laying on paint thickly) technique and executed some memorable portraits in this style. After a time, his figuration started becoming increasingly abstract. This was, perhaps, a precursor of what was to follow soon. Santosh would often recall that in the year 1964, during a visit to the holy Amarnath cave in south Kashmir, he was deeply touched by something. This was perhaps a touch of divine grace. After an 'artistic silence' for a time, he started painting in what came to be later known as the Neo-Tantric form or school. He can, in fact, be considered to be among the founders of this school. He continued to paint in this style till his death on March 10, 1997. This style of painting at once defines and describes the artistic persona of Ghulam Rasool Santosh.

Santosh built his personal world as well as his world of art around Kashmir Shaivite philosophy, commonly referred to as *tantra* philosophy. *Tantra* literally means expansion and refers to a body of text (*tantra shastras*) which are part of the *agama* (divinely revealed) *shastras* (texts). There are Buddhist *tantra* texts as well, which are partly derivative. The great Indian philosopher and aesthetician, Abhinavagupta, who incidentally was from Kashmir, prepared a comprehensive listing of the *tantra* text with an exhaustive commentary entitled *Tantraloka*. In practice *tantra* has two manifestations – the aural, known as *mantra*; and the visual, known as *yantra*. Both are well documented. In fact there are as many as 960 *yantras* that have been mentioned. This could well be classified as *tantric* art. Since the art of Santosh and some other exponents, though influenced by it, is not in strict accordance with the prescribed format of *yantras*, it has come to be known as the Neo-Tantric (as distinct from *tantric*) school of art. This nomenclature is, at best, broadly indicative.

It is important to understand the basis of this seemingly esoteric philosophy and its aesthetic implications in some detail to fully understand the artistic vision of Santosh. Kashmir Shaiva philosophy, also known as the *ardha-tryambaka* school of Shaivism, is different from other schools of Indian philosophy, even other Shaiva schools. It understands existence on the microcosmic as well as macrocosmic levels. It also considers the physical body to be a vehicle for the attainment of self-realisation. It recommends the use of *mantra* or chanting – consisting mostly of phonemes rather than words – and the contemplation of *yantra* or the visual – a schematic visual stimulus – for *sadhana* (meditation). This is supposed to uncoil and raise the inherent energy (*kundalini shakti* – energy that is wound like a coiled serpent) from its basic somnolent level (*mooladhara chakra* – level of the basic foundation), through several intermediate stages, to its highest level (*sahasrar* or *sahasra kamaldal* – cluster of a thousand lotuses), resulting in the attainment of self-realisation.

Kashmir Shaiva philosophy is concerned with the notion of number-related geometry and phoneme-related vocalisation besides the assigning of different values of the colour spectrum to various states of being and experience. This is of particular interest in trying to understand the evolution of Santosh's art. It is the practice of *sadhana*, however, that is the experiential level of

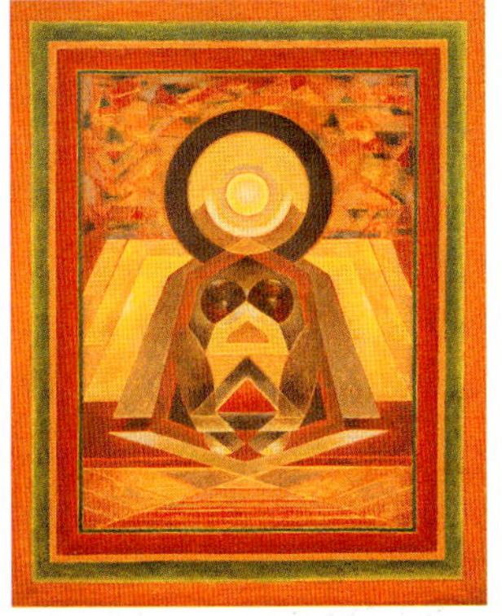

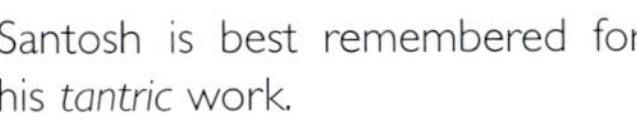

Santosh is best remembered for his *tantric* work.

understanding. Santosh underwent a formal initiation into the *krama* (incremental) way, one of the three sub-schools of Kashmir Shaivism and practiced *sadhana* for many years. His artistic output during this time chronicled and, in fact, echoed his continuing personal evolution. The geometrically precise and symmetrical compositions were seemingly structured in the manner of classical *mandala*s or *yantra*s, yet they were neither. An alchemy took place and the notional was transformed into something powerfully immediate and real. Colour was no longer merely an assigned value, form not only notational. Here colour was an individually felt light and on occasion, sound.

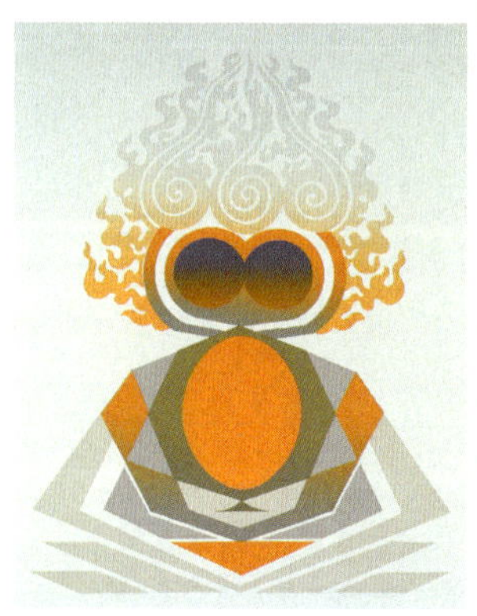

Creating his own *mantra* and *yantra.*

Kashmir Shaiva philosophy distinguishes between *yantra* – the visual, geometric state and *mantra* – signs or symbols. It is up to the *sadhaka* (meditator) to merge the two creatively. Santosh created his own *mantra* and his own *yantra* in his poetry and other writings as well as in his art, drawing upon the same matrix.

Santosh was an acclaimed poet and writer in Kashmiri in addition to being a celebrated artist. He received the Sahitya Akademi Award in 1979 for his book of poems *Besukh Ruh*, besides receiving the Padma Shri in 1977 and the Kalhana Award in 1985. He received the National Award for Painting in 1958 for the first time and twice subsequently: the Sahitya Kala Parishad Artist of the Year Award in 1984, and the apex award of the All India Fine Arts and Craft Society (AIFACS). His paintings are in many prestigious collections worldwide. His art has been on view at major expositions and has travelled to New York, Kabul, Tel Aviv, Chicago, Los Angeles, Cairo, Zurich, Honolulu, Tokyo, Dubai, Manila, Montreal and other places.

An analysis of the art of Santosh, particularly the so-called Neo-Tantric work, reveals many interesting technical aspects. The first thing one notices is that the pictorial space is vertically bisected and the images on either side of this imaginary divide are reflections of each other – exact, symmetrical, laterally reversed reflections. In other words, each composition is a conjunction of twin mirror images. Another fact that one notices is the invariable presence of a multiple border, giving the canvas an uncanny feel of a window or a casement without actually representing that. The pictorial elements are mostly a circle (numeral value of infinity), *bindu* or point (numeral value of 1), a straight line (value 2), a triangle (value 3), a pentagon (value 5), a *shatkon* (hexangle) in the form of two overlapping triangles or a six-pointed star (value 6) and polygons of higher order. The numeral value of these higher polygons is mostly in configurations of 9, 12, 18, 26 and 36. All these numerals have a special significance in Kashmir Shaiva philosophy. Here *Param Shiva* (ultimate reality) is the essential *tattva* (attribute) of all creation, *prakriti* (Nature) and its thirty-six elements. The numeral 36 inherently represents geometry and geometrical forms. Six multiplied by three is eighteen, half of thirty-six, signifying the eighteen formalised attributes of Shakti – her arms. Also, six and three are nine – only a quarter of thirty-six. This quarter is the *nav yoni mandala* (nine levels of existence). This is represented by the geometrical configuration of three triangles. Rectangles and other quadrilaterals make an appearance but rarely, while the oval – representing *hiranyagarbha* or the celestial ovum – recurs most frequently. While these geometric shapes occur in two dimensions, their construction and positioning suggests the third dimension. Thus the triangle becomes a pyramid, the square a cube and so forth. The higher polygonal structures become complex crystals. Sometimes one is reminded of a stained-glass window with a million tiny pieces

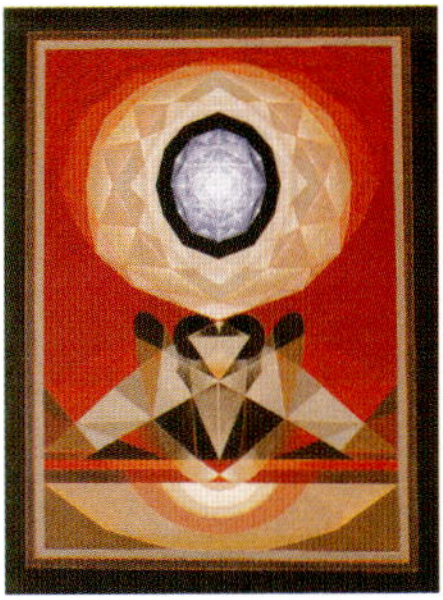

The merging of geometric shapes creates a third dimension in his work.

of stained glass put together according to some magical formula pertaining to their chromatic value, glittering gemlike and looking like a diadem of light. Curvilinear forms make an appearance in the later works giving rise to cloud-like formations. This gives the feel of a Tibetan *thanka* to some of these works.

Viewed from a certain perspective most of Santosh's Neo-Tantric paintings look like stylised portraits of the female form, seated in *padmasana* (the lotus position). This is no mere coincidence. There is a definite suggestion of the female torso in the placement of geometric elements within the composition. This stylisation is symptomatic of the devotion of Santosh for Shakti, the Divine Mother. Santosh wrote *Shakti Vichara* in 1980, a long poem in the hallowed tradition of the epic *Bhawani Sahasranama*, dwelling exclusively on Shakti in her various manifestations.

Santosh was a superb colourist. His competence in handling colour with varying degrees of delicacy or vigour was evident right from his earliest work, regardless of the medium. He was equally at home with watercolour, oil and later, acrylic. His attempt at creating the feeling of light was quite visible even in early works. With his uniquely individual fusion of the structural with the chromatic, he was able to achieve it later with great success. His palette, while routinely incorporating the assigned colours of *tantric* practice like vermilion and black, incorporated a wide spectrum. He was not daunted by pigments most other artists would have shied away from since he had supreme confidence in his own ability to handle them. And his confidence was certainly not misplaced. Greens and yellows co-existed with crimson

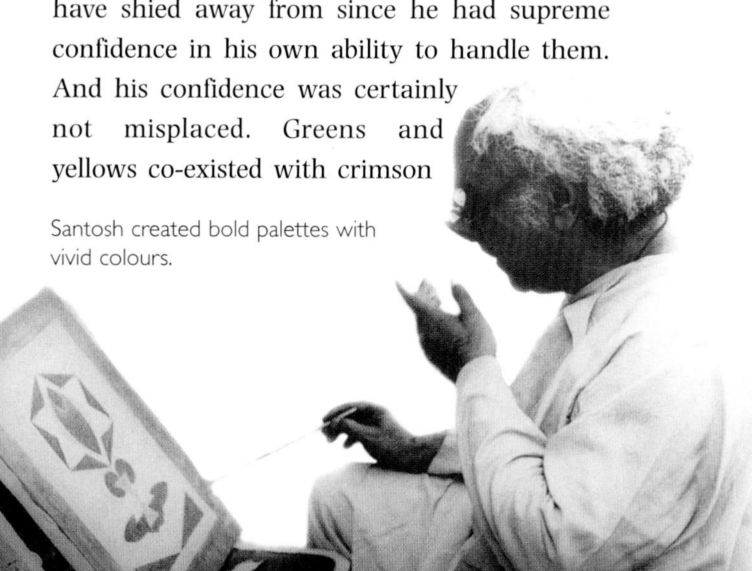

Santosh created bold palettes with vivid colours.

and vermilion in perfect harmony at any level of saturation. Santosh once said during an interview, 'I don't sketch, I divide the canvas down the central axis and start. Since I try to create colour as light, the painting is built slowly, gradually.' Again, 'People respond spontaneously. They see the work. I tell them to take time over it. And they come around, by many routes, to the same basic point – linking these paintings to the contemplative life, to the practice of *yoga-sadhana*. It is the feel of the iconography; in temples, at shrines, they are in contact with it.'

An artist makes an ideal reality visible. The communication of the realised unknown is retrieval of light from darkness. It is visualising the hidden. Designing, carving and sculpting the form of sound. This, in essence, is the relationship between *mantra* and *yantra*. Santosh was like a musician giving expression to the hidden *shruti*, giving form to sound, unfolding its mystery and capturing it by freezing it in time, in artistic equilibrium.

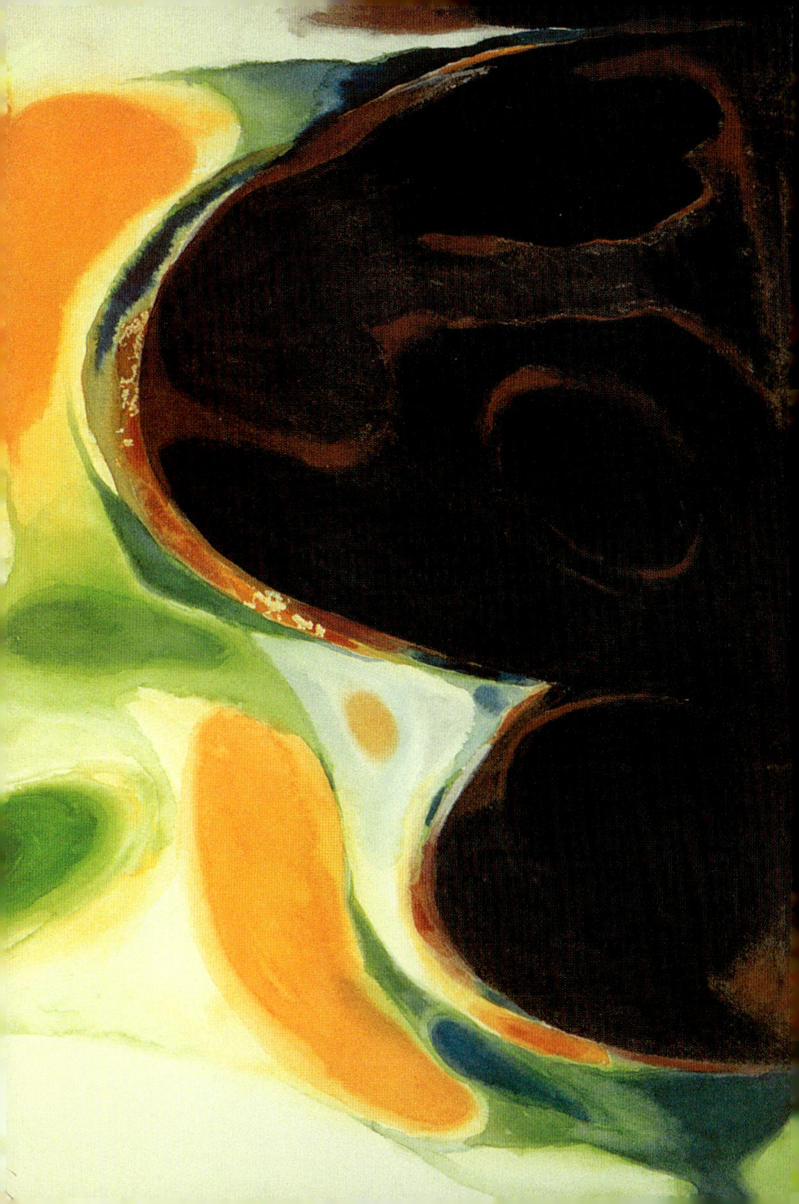

■ Reclining torso

The treatment is characteristic of much of this period. Notice the flowing colours handled with a very delicate touch.
45 x 30 cm, watercolour on paper, 1966.

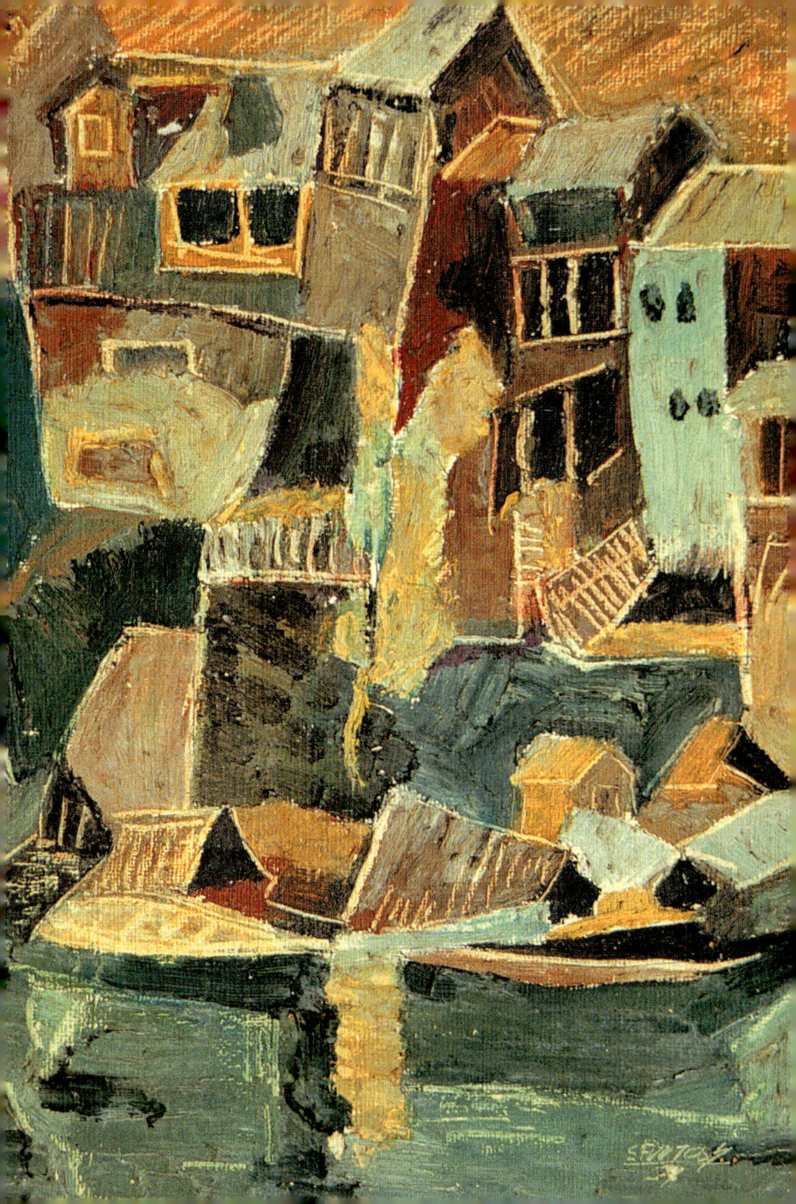

■ On the banks of the Dal Lake backwaters

36 x 26 cm, oil on soft board, 1954.

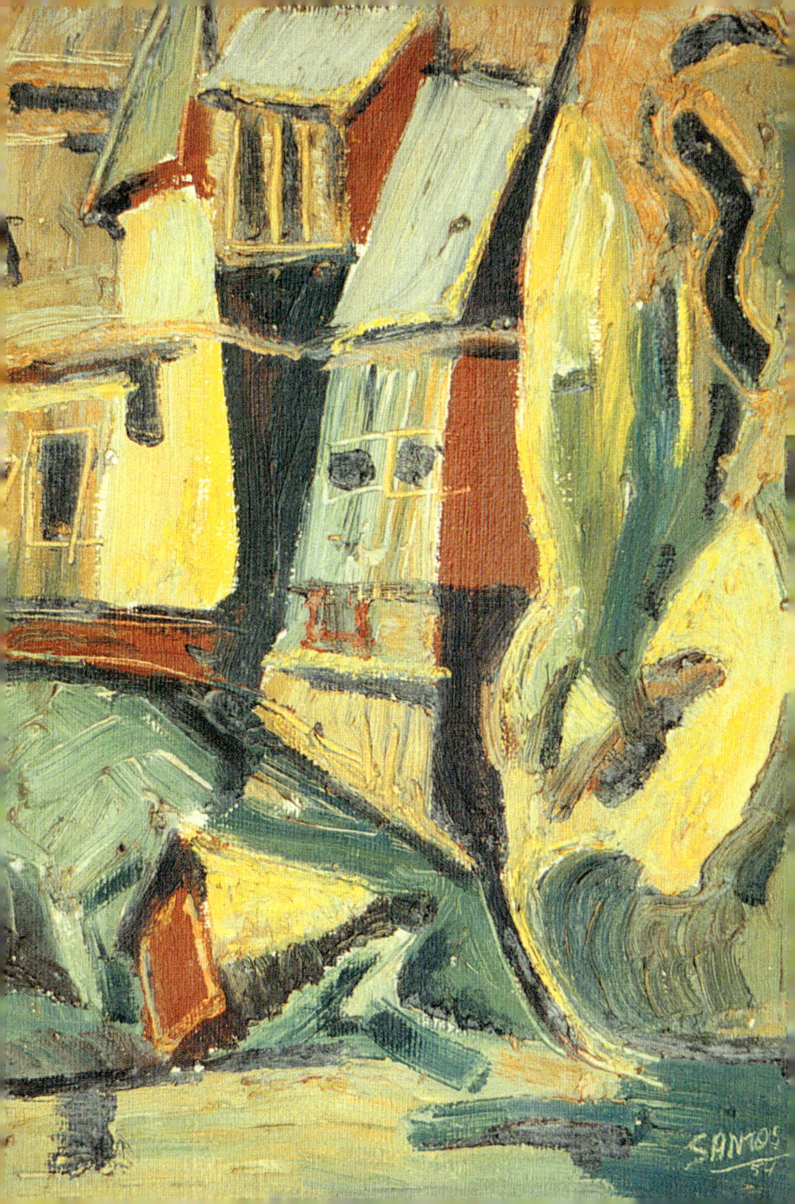
SANTOS
54

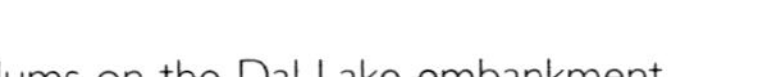

■ Slums on the Dal Lake embankment

36 x 26 cm, oil on soft board, 1954.

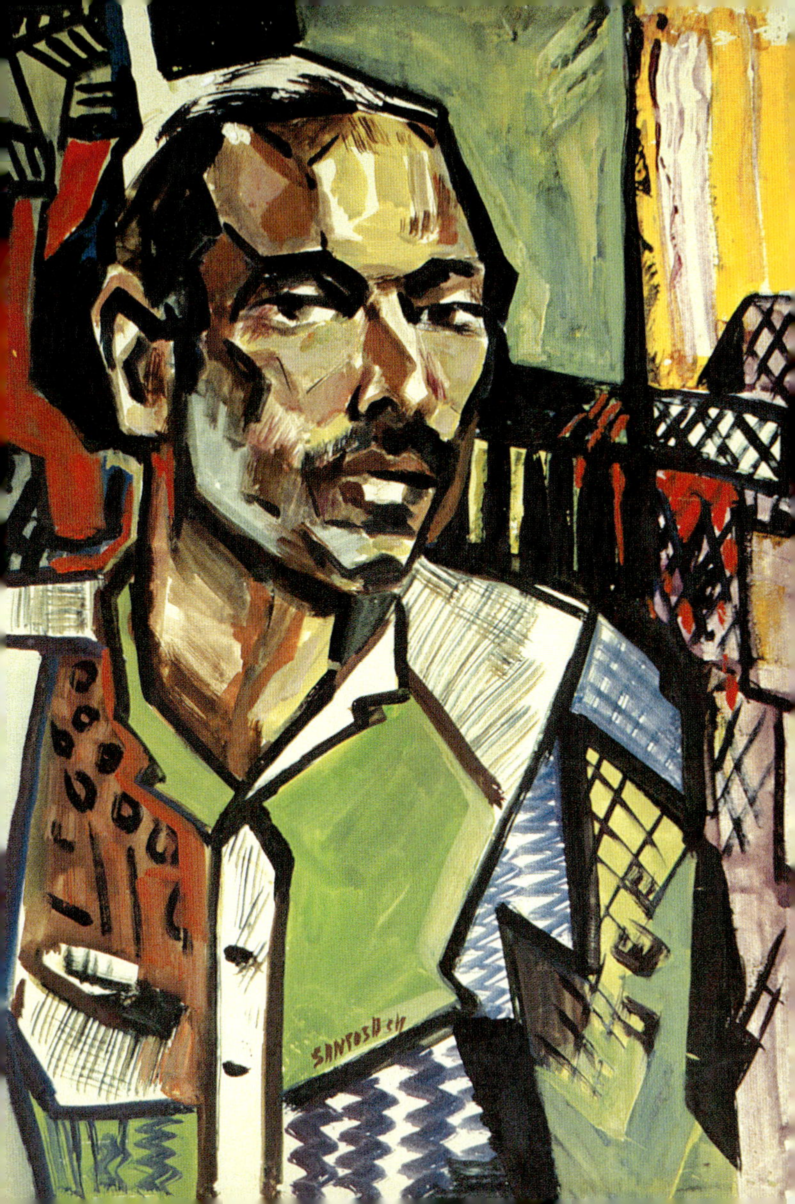
SANTOSH

■ Self-portrait

In the mould of Picasso. 54 x 38 cm, gouache on paper, 1954.

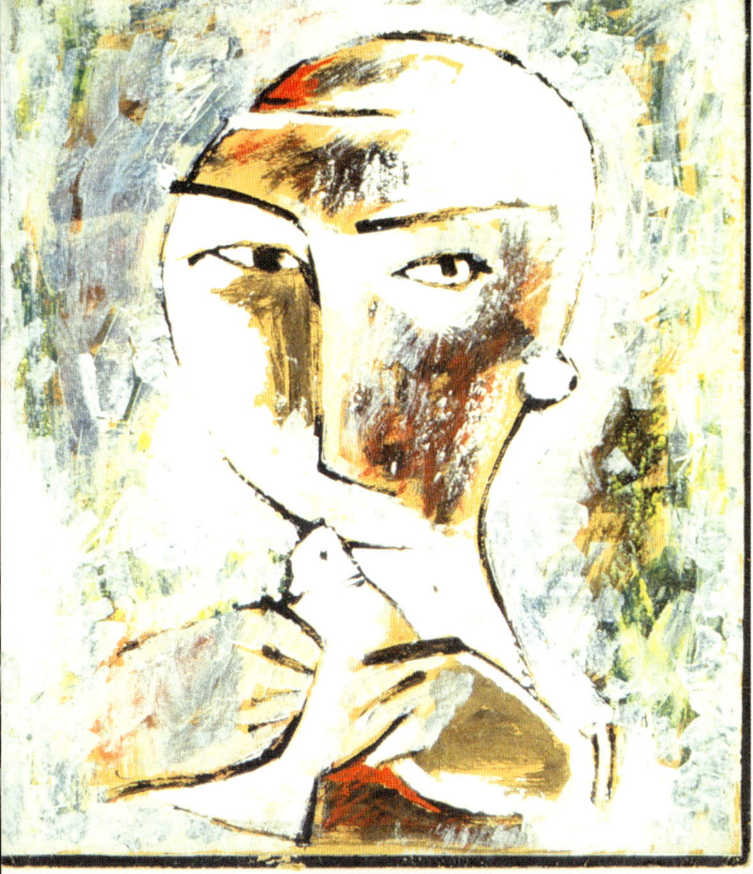

■ Girl holding a dove

37 x 42 cm, gouache on soft board, 1956.

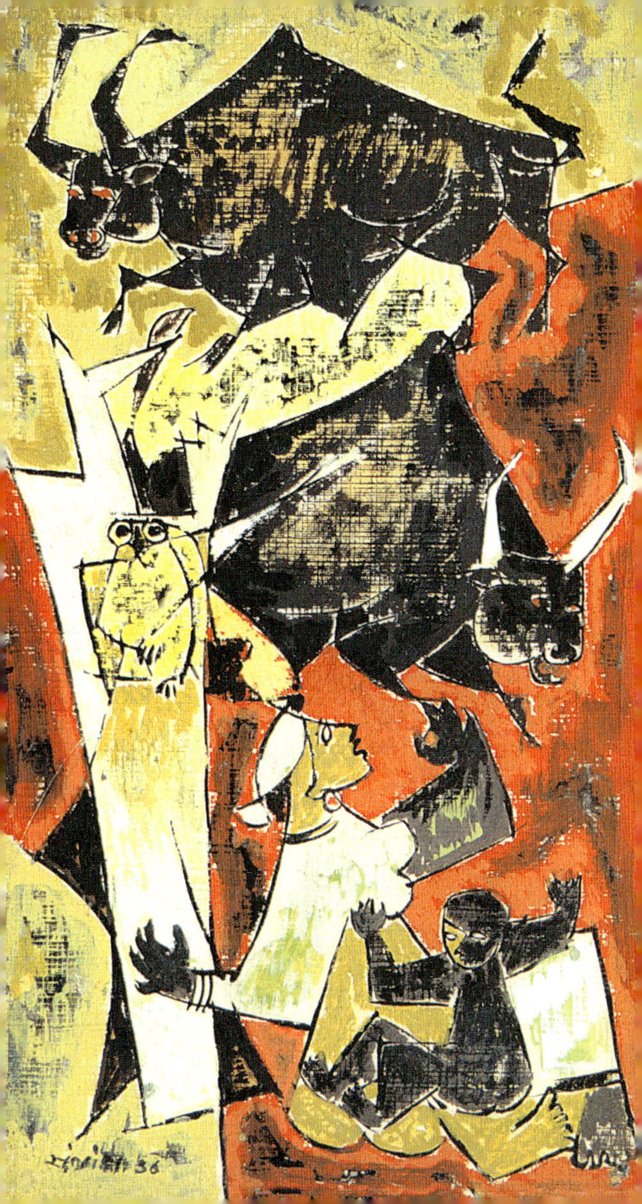

■ Allegory

14 x 26 cm, gouache on soft board, 1956.

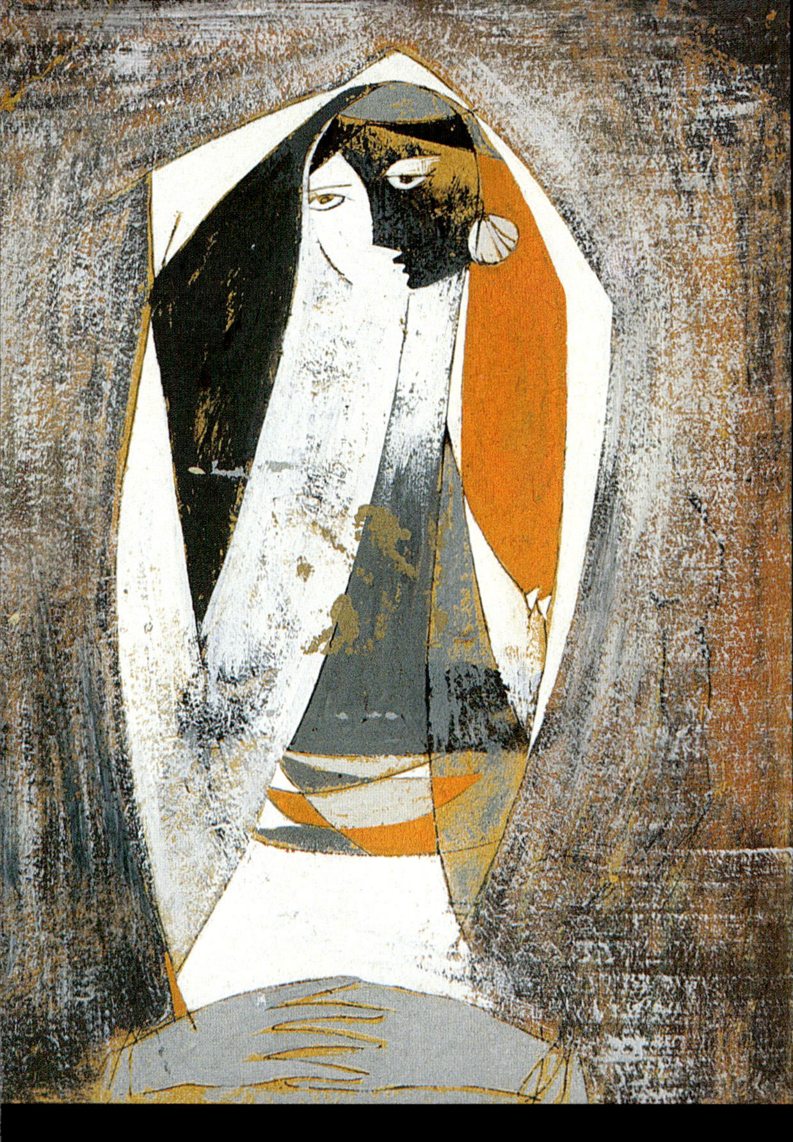

■ Portrait of a belle

19 x 24 cm, gouache on soft board, 1956.

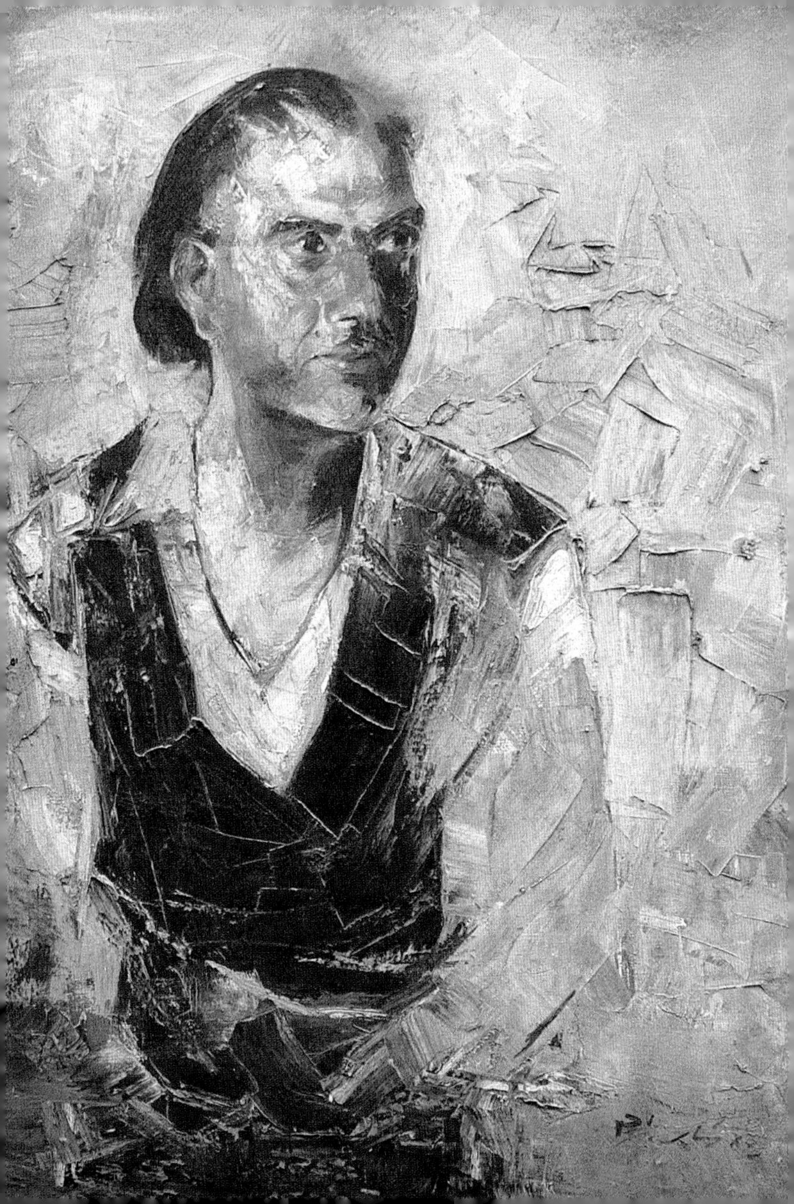

■ Nadim

Portrait of a celebrated Kashmiri poet and writer, Dinanath Nadim, in impasto style. 78 x 105 cm, oil on canvas, 1962.

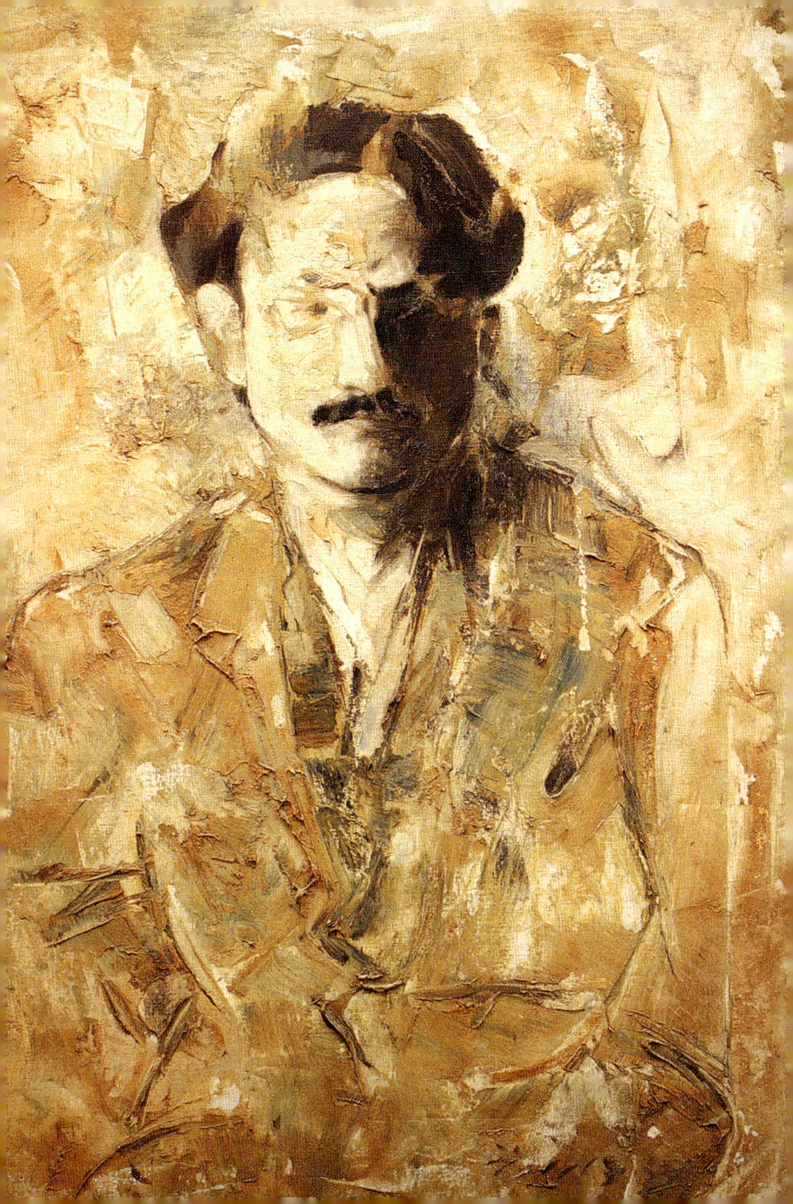

■ Triloke

Portrait of fellow artist and friend Triloke Kaul executed in the impasto style.
78 x 103 cm, oil on canvas, 1963.

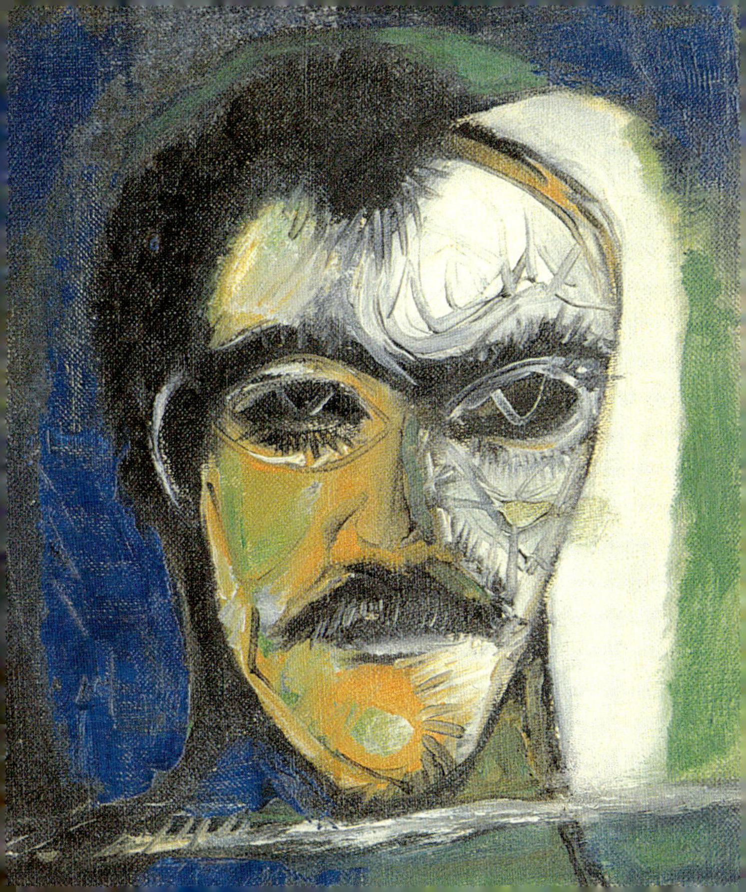

■ Self-portrait

In the mould of Salvador Dali. 20 x 24 cm, oil on canvas, 1966.

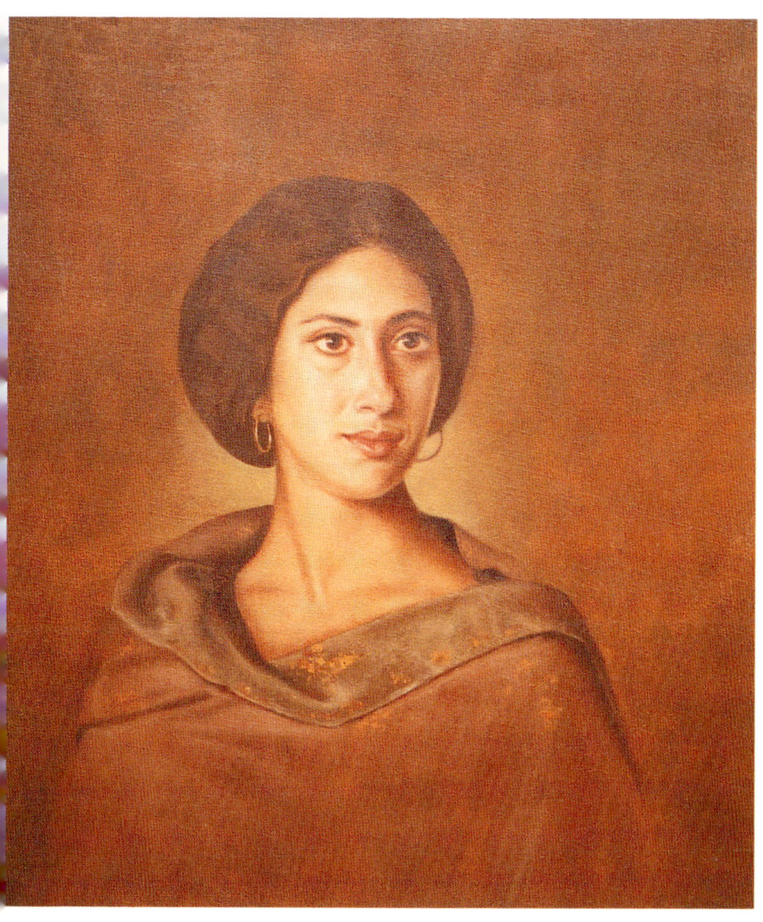

■ Sharon

A classical portrait of the famous danseuse Sharon Lowen. 64 x 76 cm, oil on canvas, 1970.

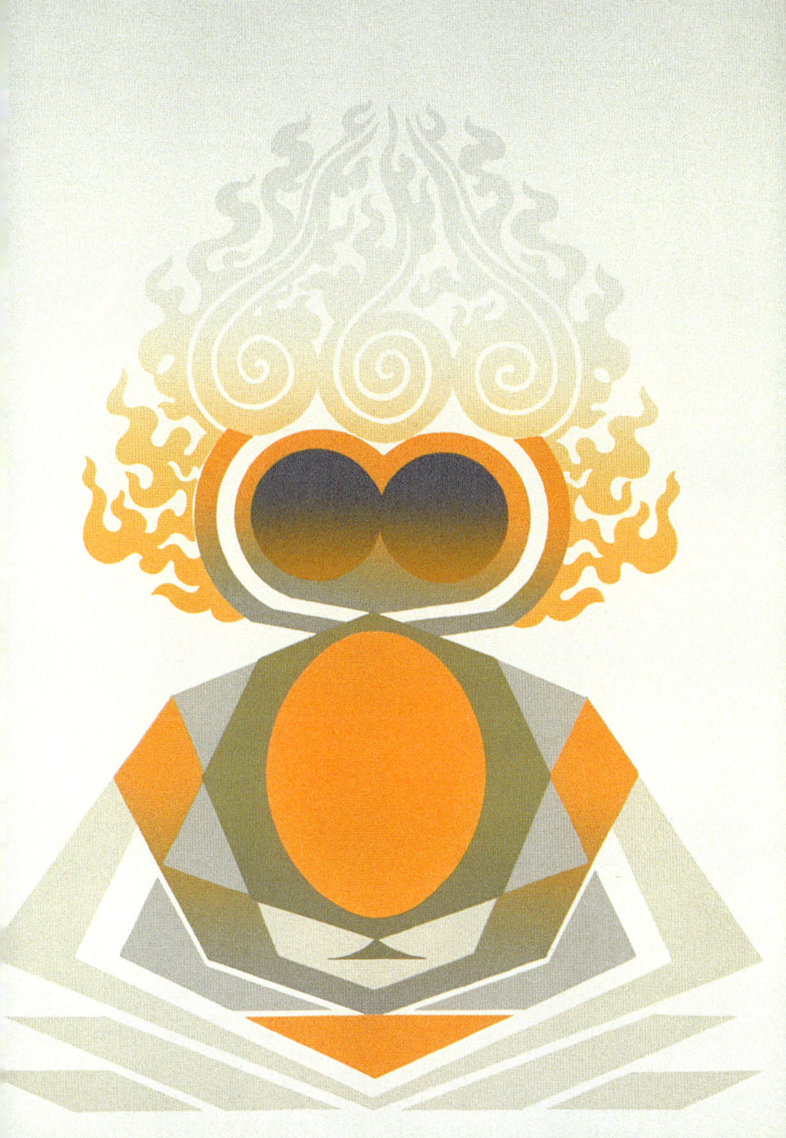

■ *Sahasrar*

61 x 45 cm, silk-screen print, 1980.

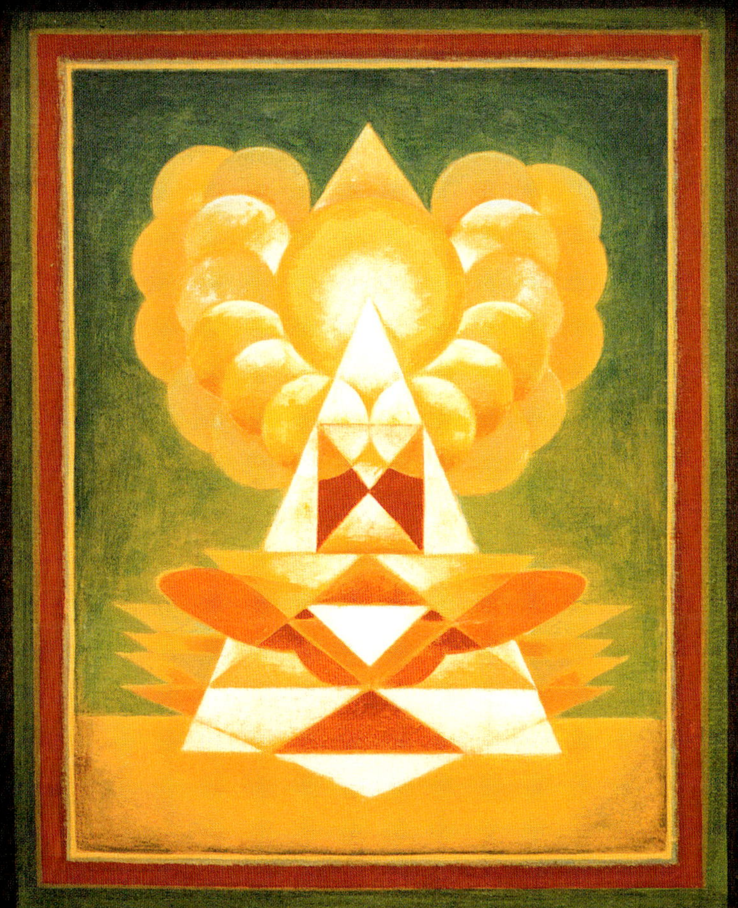

■ *Shakti vichar*

51 x 41 cm, acrylic on canvas board, 1982.

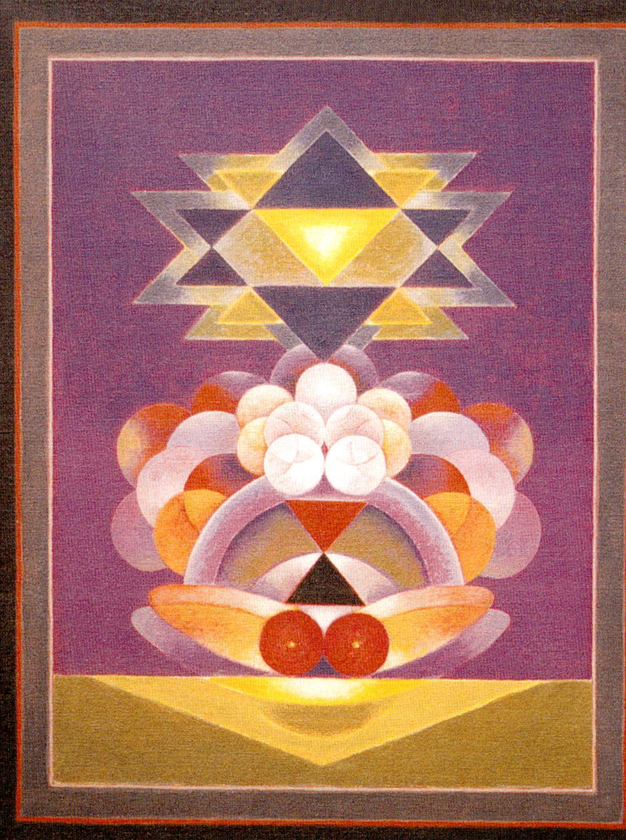

■ The solid *mandala*

61 x 78 cm, acrylic on canvas, 1984.

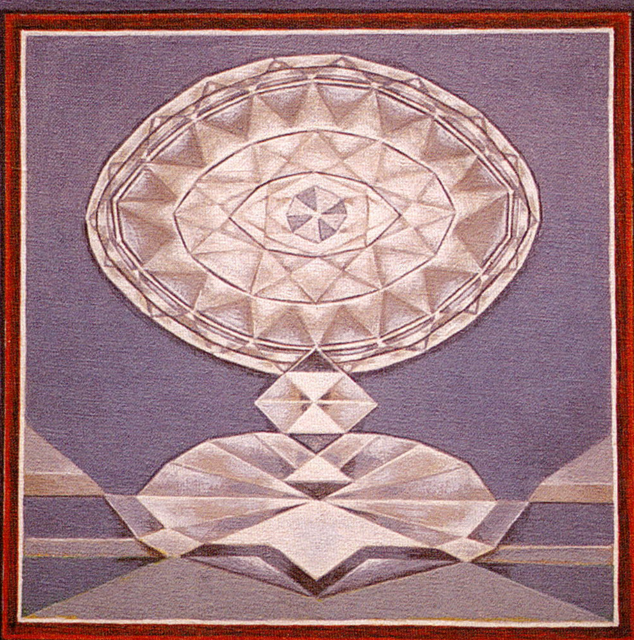

■ Crystal *yantra*

33 x 33 cm, acrylic on canvas, 1990.

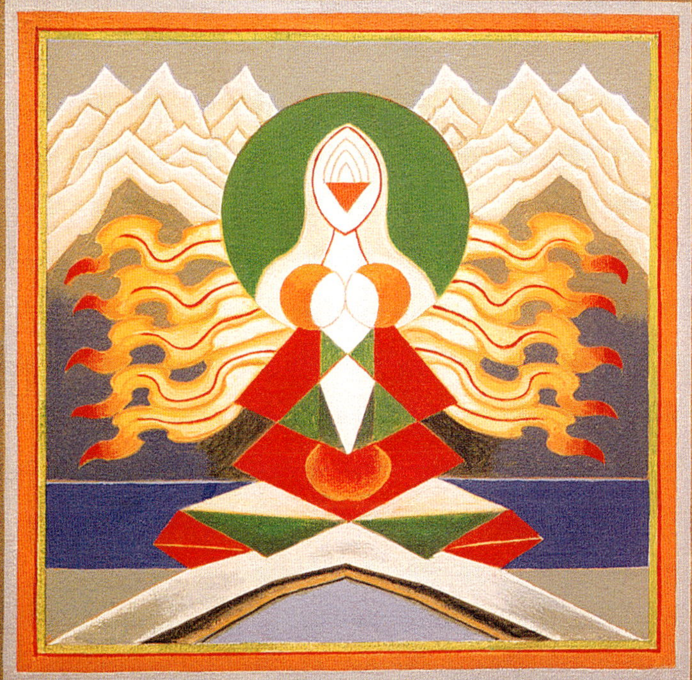

■ The elements within

45 x 45 cm, acrylic on canvas, 1990.

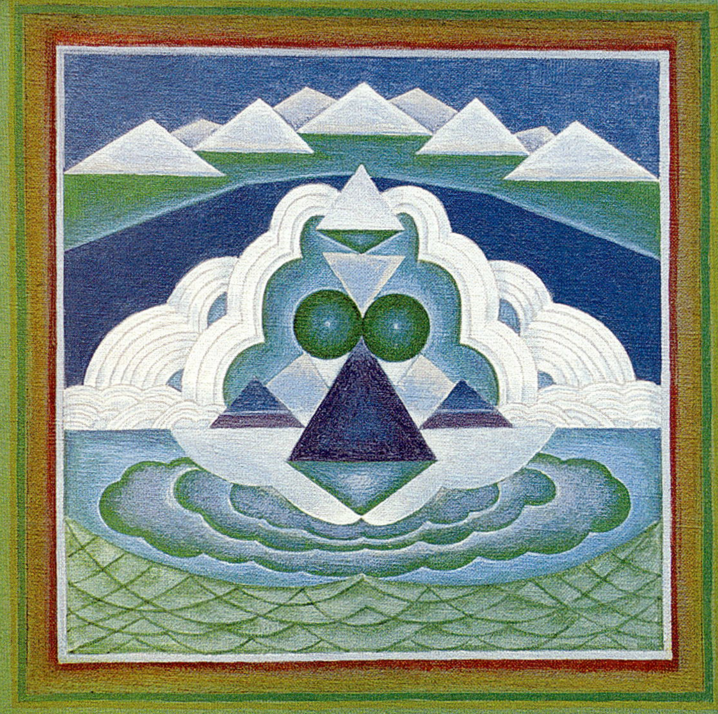

■ Water

Part of the series on Pancha Mahabhuta – *the five basic elements.* 29 x 29 cm, acrylic on canvas, 1990.

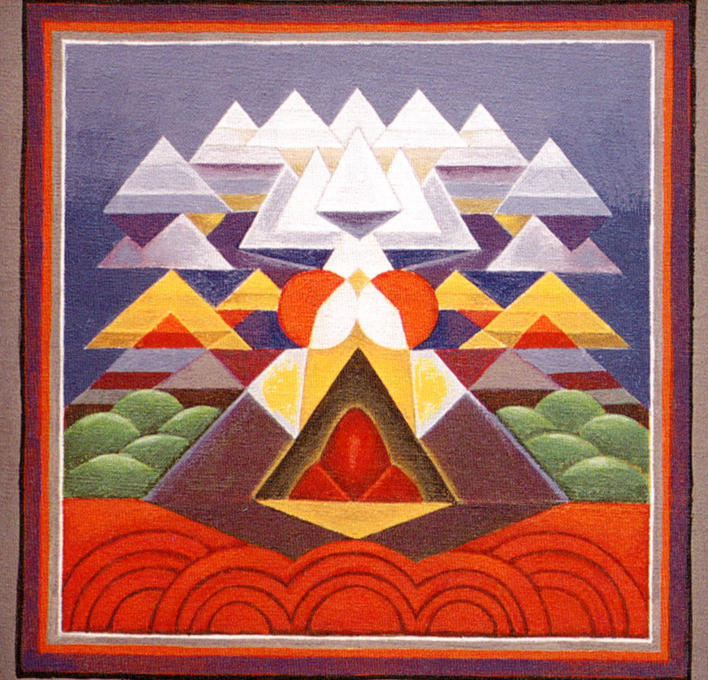

■ Earth

Another work in the Pancha Mahabhuta *series.* 29 x 29 cm, acrylic on canvas, 1990.

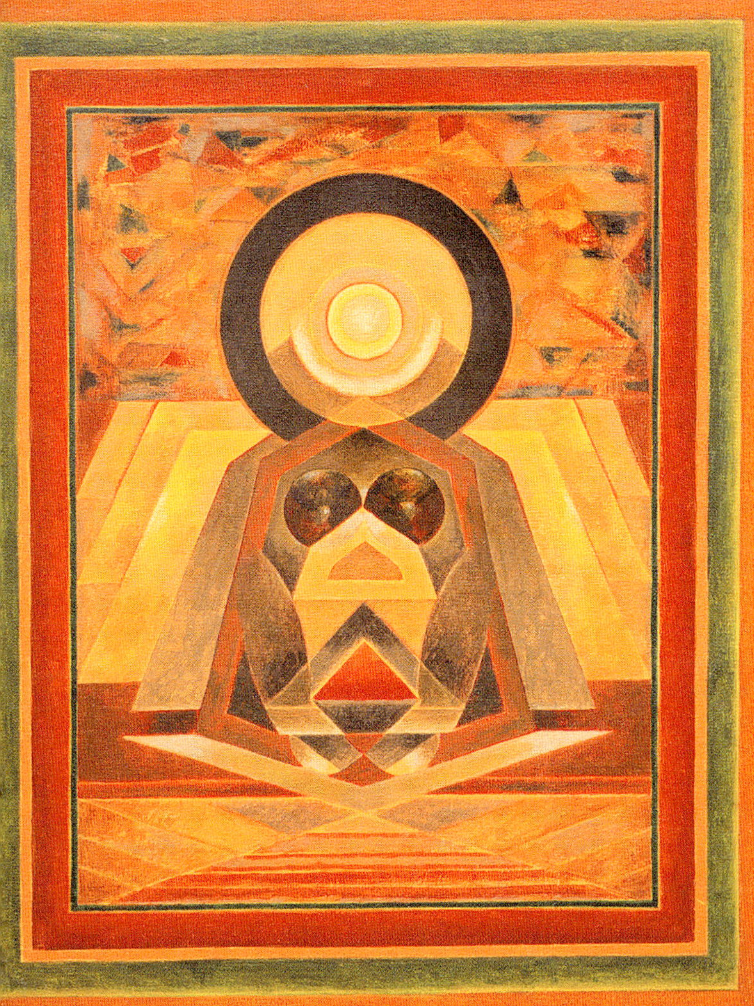

■ *Vishwaroopa*

61 x 76 cm, acrylic on canvas, 1984.

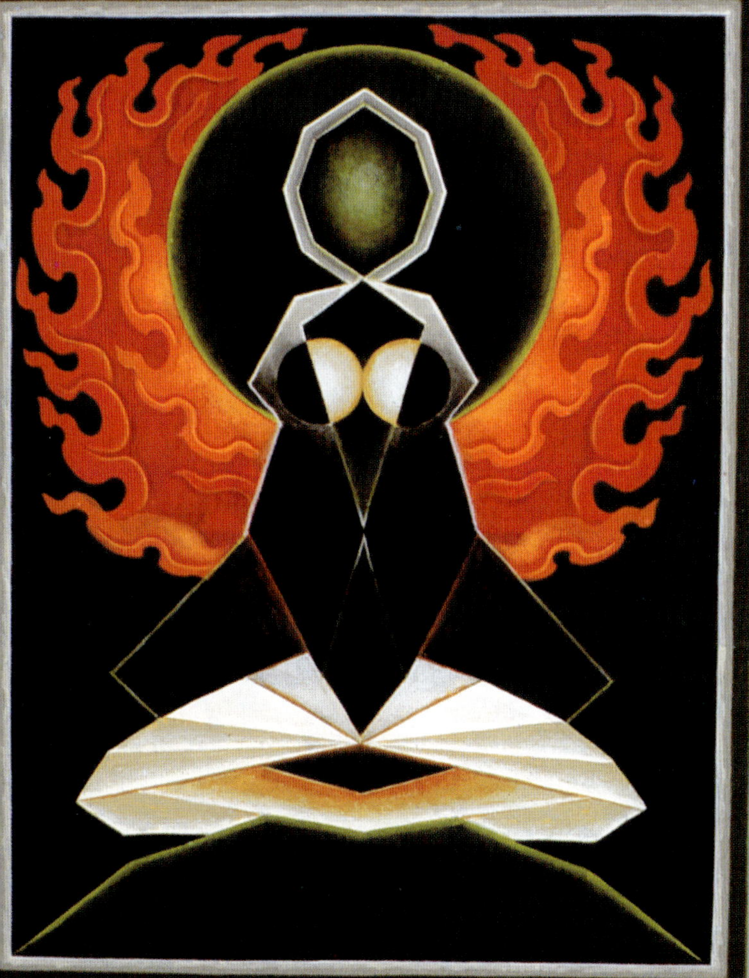

■ *Agni* (fire)

61 x 76 cm, acrylic on canvas, 1994.

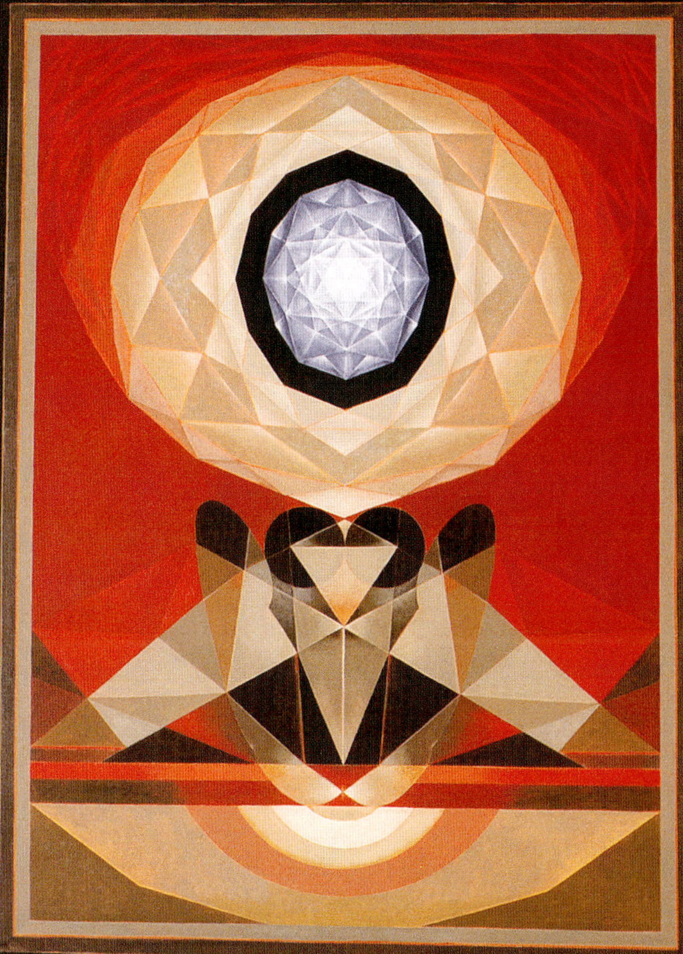

■ *Sahaja*

---

122 x 163 cm, acrylic on canvas, 1992.

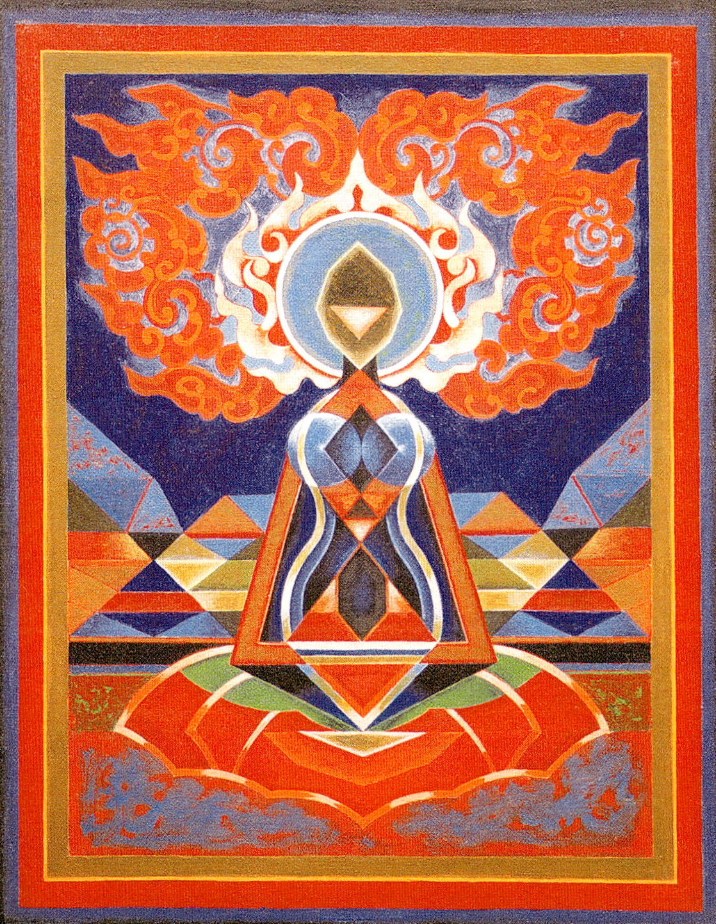

■ Nada-Brahma

61 x 76 cm, acrylic on canvas, 1996.

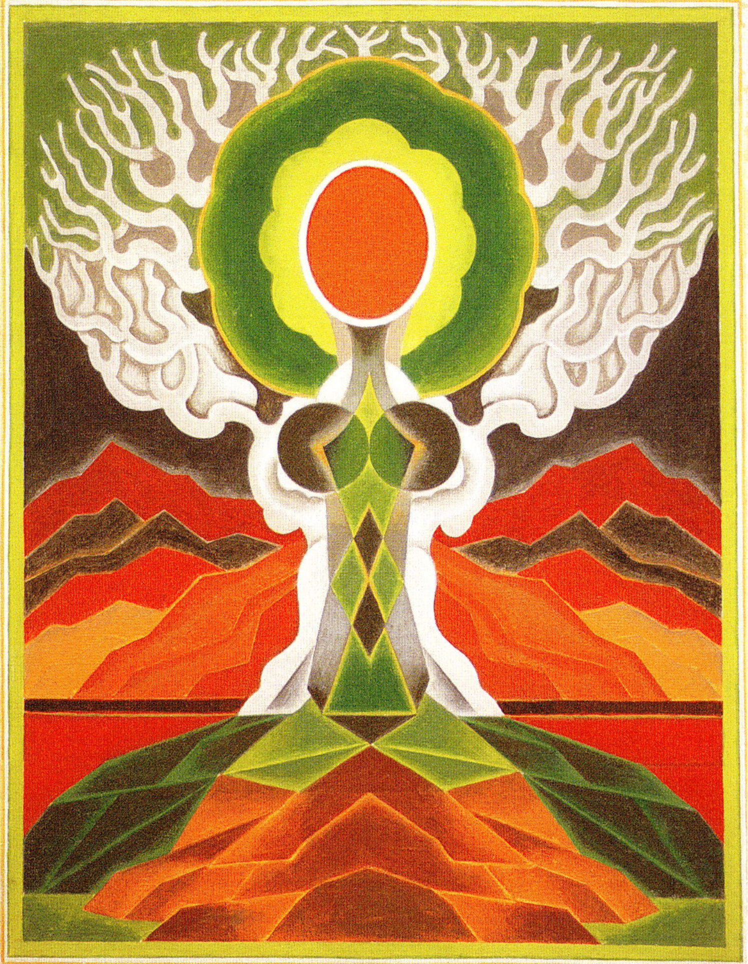

■ Effulgence

61 x 78 cm, acrylic on canvas, 1996.

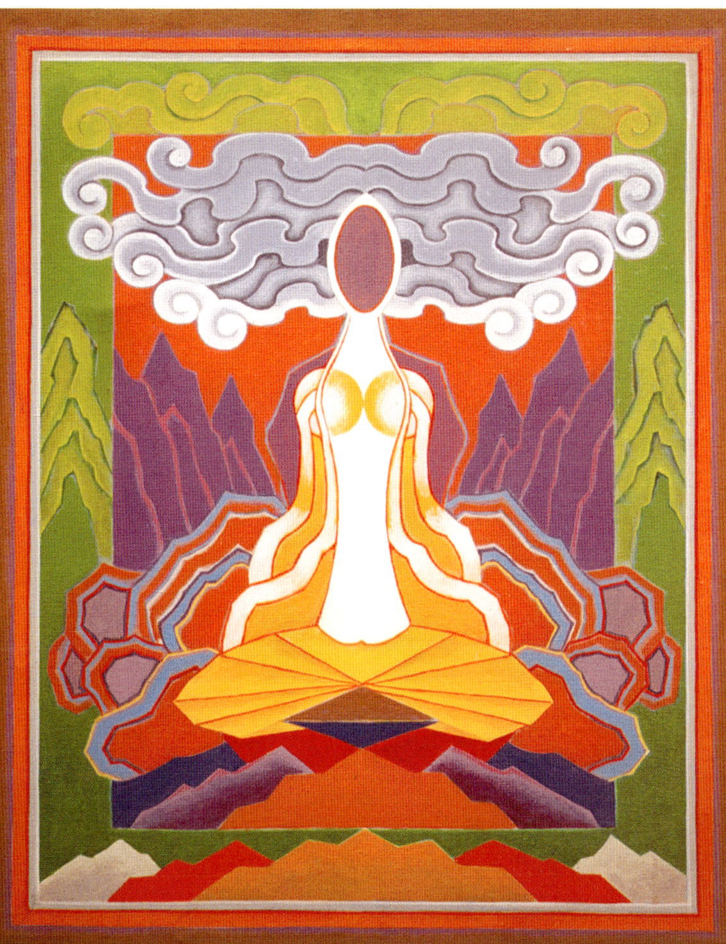

■ *Shakti-Pata*

61 x 78 cm, acrylic on canvas, 1996.

■ Front cover: Kali kalpana. 28 × 35 cm, acrylic on canvas, 1992.